5L

5L

*I dedicate this volume to the memory of*
*Prof. Süheyl Ünver, my teacher.*

Copyright © 1988 by Dover Publications, Inc.
All rights reserved under Pan American and International Copyright Conventions.

Published in Canada by General Publishing Company, Ltd., 30 Lesmill Road, Don Mills, Toronto, Ontario.
Published in the United Kingdom by Constable and Company, Ltd.

*Treasury of Turkish Designs: 670 Motifs from Iznik Pottery* is a new work, first published by Dover Publications, Inc., in 1988.

DOVER *Pictorial Archive* SERIES

Manufactured in the United States of America
Dover Publications, Inc., 31 East 2nd Street, Mineola, N.Y. 11501

*Library of Congress Cataloging-in-Publication Data*

Akar, Azade.
    Treasury of Turkish designs : 670 motifs from Iznik pottery / Azade Akar.
        p.     cm.—(Dover pictorial archives series)
    Bibliography: p.
    ISBN 0-486-25594-8
    1. Iznik pottery—Themes, motives. 2. Pottery, Turkish—Turkey—Iznik—Themes, motives. 3. Decoration and ornament—Plant forms—Turkey—Iznik. I. Title. II. Series.
    NK4340.I9A35 1988
        738.3′7—dc19                                                    87-32030
                                                                                CIP

# Acknowledgment

All the designs and motifs in this volume are derived from actual ceramic objects in the following museums and private collections:

*Austria*
    Österreichisches Museum für angewandte Kunst, Vienna

*Belgium*
    Musées Royaux d'Art et d'Histoire, Brussels

*Denmark*
    C. L. Davids Samling, Copenhagen

*Egypt*
    Museum of Islamic Art, Cairo

*France*
    Château d'Écouen, Paris
    Musée des Arts Décoratifs, Paris
    Musée du Louvre, Paris
    Musée National de Céramique, Sèvres

*Great Britain*
    Ashmolean Museum, Oxford
    Barlow Collection (now dispersed in London and Cambridge)
    British Museum, London
    Fitzwilliam Museum, Cambridge
    Victoria and Albert Museum, London

*Greece*
    Benaki Museum, Athens

*Israel*
    L. A. Mayer Memorial Institute for Islamic Art, Jerusalem

*Kuwait*
    King Faisal Center, Kuwait

*Netherlands*
    Haags Gemeentemuseum, The Hague

*Portugal*
    Museu Caluste Gulbenkian, Lisbon

*Turkey*
    Archeological Museum, Istanbul
    Collection of Hüseyin Kocabas, Istanbul
    Collection of Tevfik Kuyas, Istanbul
    Museum of Turkish and Islamic Art, Istanbul
    Topkapi Palace Museum, Istanbul

*U.S.S.R.*
    Hermitage Museum, Leningrad

*United States*
    Freer Gallery of Art, Smithsonian Institution, Washington, D.C.
    Metropolitan Museum of Art, New York

*West Germany and West Berlin*
    Hetjens-Museum, Düsseldorf
    Museum für Islamische Kunst (Staatliche Museen, Preussischer Kulturbesitz), Berlin
    Museum für Kunsthandwerk, Frankfurt am Main

# Introduction

ALL THE DESIGNS and motifs included in this volume are derived from the decoration of Ottoman Turkish underglaze-painted pottery made in the city of Iznik from the late fifteenth to the mid-seventeenth centuries. Held in particularly high esteem by Western collectors for the last two hundred years, these pieces are rarely found on the antique market and remain expensive collector's items.

Today, most of these vessels have left Turkey and are scattered in museums all over the world. In my research, I have been able to locate and catalogue approximately 3000 pieces consisting of large plates, dishes, bowls, jugs, bottles, vases, mosque lamps and tankards. The whereabouts of numerous artefacts remains a mystery, since many are in private collections or housed in museums inaccessible to me. I would estimate that an additional 1000 such pieces could be located. Thus, the Iznik pottery surviving into the present probably amounts to about 4000 items in all. The plates and bowls vary from 26 cm (10¼ inches) to 43 cm (17 inches) in diameter. The designs presented here were carefully chosen from among the catalogued pieces according to styles and motifs.

It should be emphasized that this book is not intended to give a strict historical outline of this period in pottery design, but rather to serve as an inspiration to contemporary artists. In their photographs and essays, art historians often reveal only the underlying structure of a past work of art, without giving the reader a feeling for the practical use of the material. The idea here is to move away from the lifeless mission of so much traditional criticism, interested mainly in history, and instead to show and analyze the Iznik designs themselves. As the British connoisseur Sir Henry Gardner has written: "The Turkish pottery of Iznik can claim to be the most decorative and colorful pottery ever made."

The Turkish pottery dealt with in this book was made in Iznik (the ancient Nicaea) in northwestern Anatolia (Asia Minor) between 1475 and 1660 in the period of the Ottoman Empire.

Turkish tribes had dwelt on the central and northeast Asian steppes from earliest recorded times. During the eleventh century A.D., certain groups moved westward, imposing their rule on countries that had earlier been converted to Islam by the Arabs. The Seljuk Turks took Anatolia from the East Roman Empire of Byzantium, founding the Kingdom of Rum, which dissolved after 1300. But the nation was gradually reconstituted by another Turkish tribe, the Ottomans, whose empire grew steadily, with Istanbul (formerly Constantinople) as its capital after 1453. The Ottoman Empire became one of the mightiest political forces of the late Middle Ages, its boundaries eventually stretching from India, through the whole Middle East and North Africa, to much of southeastern Europe. The Empire declined severely in the nineteenth century and was extinguished after the First World War, Turkey itself (Anatolia and a small European enclave) becoming a republic.

Art flourished in tandem with the increasing wealth of the Empire. Architecture in particular experienced a renaissance as monumental palaces and mosques were erected, and the decorative arts became increasingly significant as it became fashionable to adorn the interiors of these grand buildings with ceramic tiles. In particular, the magnificent glazed tiles of Iznik came to surpass all rivals in the Middle East in brilliance of technique. Their low-fired material was composed of white clay and glassy matter with a carefully prepared porcelain-like surface on which patterns were painted before a transparent alkaline glaze was applied.

The increasing demand made Iznik a large and richly productive area where hundreds of artists were employed to produce tiles in panels and in other large-scale combinations. The designs painted on these tiles were created mainly by the palace art studios in Istanbul, and then sent to Iznik. From there the finished tiles were shipped all over the country. In Turkey today, more than 100,000 high-quality Iznik tiles are still as bright and fresh as the day they were first removed from their kilns in the sixteenth century. The Istanbul Blue Mosque alone has over 20,000 tiles on its upper floors!

The same Iznik workshops produced the pottery that is the subject of this volume. Color and design were similar to those used for tile, yet there are certain important differences. The pottery designs were produced in Iznik itself by local artists rather than by the Istanbul court designers. As a result, patterns differ slightly, exhibiting a stronger folk quality. Moreover, some of the designs used on pottery—for example, human figures, animals, fantasy creatures and sailing ships—do not occur on the tiles.

Iznik pottery may be divided historically into the following periods:

## 1. Blue-and-white period (1475–1510)

On vessels of this type, the painting is conceived in terms of small, very detailed patterns with fine lines and intricate shading. The individual motifs, densely combined, recall the Ottoman illuminated manuscripts, whose designs also reveal the effects of a strong Chinese and Central Asian influence. The pottery designs are strongly highlighted in a blue of consistent technical brilliance, skillfully applied in shades of varying strength. Motifs are painted on a white background or applied in dark blue lines on a medium or light blue background. The glaze is lustrous, very thin and close-fitting.

## 2. Blue-turquoise-white period (1500–1520)

The designs are quite similar to those of the first period, but are affected by the introduction of a first pale, then brilliant, turquoise. A black outline surrounding the turquoise motifs occasionally appears. In addition, the designs get larger, with flower and leaf motifs composed in a manner more fitting to the decoration of pottery. Occasionally there are animal motifs.

## 3. So-called Damascus group (1520–1555)

These wares were once erroneously believed to have been made in Damascus, a part of the Ottoman Empire at that time, because many tiles of the period were actually acquired there. However, it has been proven that the patrons in Damascus actually ordered these wall tiles from Iznik to use in decorating their buildings. This series of tiles and vessels, perhaps the most inventive in Iznik history, adds new colors to the palette and features luxuriant seminaturalistic plant ornamentation. The motifs, which become large and bold, include roses, tulips, carnations, pomegranates, feathery leaves and trees. Among the purely decorative conventions are cloud scrolls that bind the plant stems like clasps (*agraf* in Turkish) and the highly stylized *hatayi* and *rumi* motifs (see below) scattered or spiraling among the seminaturalistic flower designs. Characteristic colors are olive green, pale pink, turquoise, cobalt blue, purple, brown and gray.

## 4. So-called Rhodian group (1550–1600)

This best-known and most abundant type of Iznik pottery was formerly believed to have been manufactured on the Greek island of Rhodes, because a collection of about 600 pieces of this type of pottery was brought from Rhodes to the Musée de Cluny in Paris in the nineteenth century. Although this assumption was later proven false, the name has stuck.

This is pottery of a very high quality using slip and underglaze painting on white clay. The soft "Damascus" colors were discarded in favor of the "Rhodian" hues. The black for outlining motifs becomes very intense, while the copper green, ultramarine blue and tomato red that make this pottery so famous are introduced in this period. The intense scarlet stands out in perceptible relief under the glaze, adding a three-dimensional design element of its own.

The designs follow the tradition of the "Damascus" period but new, peculiar motifs also appear at this time. All kinds of animal motifs, birds, fantastic creatures such as harpies and dragons, galleons and other sailing ships and geometrical motifs are often used. The floral designs become quite naturalistic, with large leaves.

## 5. Early seventeenth-century wares (1600–1660)

Manufacture in Iznik continued into the seventeenth century but after 1600 the quality of the pottery deteriorated appreciably. The glaze became poorer, the background got dirty and the colors lost their brilliance. Yet the designs followed the tradition of the old ones with a few new groups of motifs included. The human figures, designs of buildings and caricatural animals were produced in this period.

Manufacture finally ceased at the end of the seventeenth century.

Among the thousands of Iznik pieces distributed all over the world, one rarely encounters two vessels of identical design. Sometimes a plate and a bowl form a set or, as illustrated on page 83, there appear to be plates produced in sets. Yet, even in these matching plates, the inner designs are distinctive.

The motifs used in Iznik pottery can be grouped as follows:

1. Motifs showing a strong Chinese influence.
   (a) The rock-and-wave motif, generally serving as the outer border on plates, was very fashionable and frequently used.
   (b) Cloud motifs in all varieties.
   (c) Chinese lotus flowers and the like.
2. A highly stylized motif based on animal and bird forms—the *rumi*. The Western world labeled such motifs "arabesques." They originated in Central Asia and were used as a favorite ornamental style throughout the Islamic world. Sometimes the designs seem to have deteriorated, and look like leaves or flowers.*
3. Another broad group of motifs is called *hatayi*. These are floral motifs so highly stylized that no particular species is recognizable. They are elaborate palmettes, curving leaves or rosettes of complex design.†
4. Seminaturalistic flower designs of the "Damascus" period.
5. Naturalistic flower designs of the "Rhodian" period.

---

*Etymologically, *rumi* means "Roman," referring first to the Byzantine (Eastern Roman) Empire and later to the European lands of the Ottoman Empire. *Rumi* designs have also been described as consisting of elongated leaves with pointed tips, forming scrolls or cartouches.

†Etymologically, *hatayi* has been taken to mean "Cathayan," "Central Asian" or "from Hatay" (a Turkish administrative district on the south coast of Asia Minor). *Hatayi* designs have also been described as stylized lotus blossoms.

6. Dagger leaves, which are long, serrated, feathery leaves that sometimes dominate the entire painting on the vessel. These designs, used very often, were known to the Turkish decorator as *saz* (literally, "reed").

7. Tree motifs, especially the cypress and the "spring tree," both having symbolic meaning in Turkish art.

8. Geometrical motifs such as nets, circles, triangles and polygons.

9. Designs beginning from a central point and forming a rosette.

10. Motifs in the form of medallions called *shamsah* ("sun[burst]").

11. Patterns used to fill up a background instead of color. The most common are the small spiral called "the snail" and the imbricated pattern sometimes called "fish scales."

12. Borders, of the most varied dimensions, which surround the main design of the vessel. They sometimes even dominate the other designs.

13. Holy-water flask, vase and ewer designs surrounded by flowers were quite popular on the "Rhodian" wares.

14. Bird designs were also popular on "Rhodian" wares.

15. Stylized animals such as the lion, tiger, wolf, bull, horse, rabbit and deer were popular, too. They are naïvely done, unaided creations of the pottery painters, but they have a definite charm.

16. Legendary and mythological beings such as the phoenix, dragon and harpies were used, though not very often. They were symbols of prosperity.

17. Sailing vessels and galleon designs.

18. Spiral patterns, sometimes called the "Golden Horn" type.

19. A pattern of three tight crescents, or "tiger dots" as they are sometimes called, quite popular throughout the entire period of Iznik wares. Called the *chintemani* motif, it was a symbol of prosperity and good fortune.*

20. Architectural motifs.

21. Fruits were not as commonly used as flowers, with the exception of grapes and pomegranates. Both symbolized paradise in Ottoman tradition.

22. Designs incorporating Christian or European symbols. They were most probably produced on order.

---

*Possible etymology: the *cintāmaṇi* ("magic gem") of Buddhist art in Central and East Asia.

NOTE: Following is the proper Turkish spelling (the form shown first) for several words and names that appear in the text in an adapted form (the form shown second). (All other forms are correct in Turkish as they stand.)

çintemani — chintemani
hatayı — hatayi
İstanbul — Istanbul
İznik — Iznik
şemse — shamsah
Topkapı — Topkapi

# For Further Reading

Aslanapa, Oktay, "Pottery and Kilns from the İznik Excavations," in *Forschungen zur Kunst Asiens,* ed. Oktay Aslanapa and Rudolph Naumann, Istanbul, 1970.

Denny, Walter B., "Ceramics," in *Turkish Art,* ed. Esin Atıl, Washington, D.C., and New York, 1980.

Lane, Arthur, "The Ottoman Pottery of Isnik," *Ars Orientalis* 2 (1957), 247–281.

Öney, Gönül, *Turkish Ceramic Tile Art,* Tokyo, 1975.

Otto-Dorn, Katharina, *Türkische Keramik,* Ankara, 1957.

Öz, Tahsin, *Turkish Ceramics,* Ankara, 1957.

Petsopoulos, Yanni, *Tulips?: Arabesques and Turbans,* London, 1982.

Rogers, J. Michael, *Islamic Art and Design,* London, 1983.

Soustiel, Jean, *La céramique islamique,* Paris, 1985; translated as *Islamic Ceramics,* New York.

*Fig. 1:* Plate with "Golden Horn" decoration.
(Musée des Arts Décoratifs, Paris)

*Fig. 2:* Plate of the blue-turquoise-white period.
(British Museum, London)

*Fig. 3:* Plate of the "Damascus" period.
(British Museum, London)

*Fig. 4:* Plate of the "Damascus" period.
(British Museum, London)

*Fig. 5:* Plate of the "Damascus" period.
(British Museum, London)

*Plate 6:* Plate of the "Damascus" period.
(Victoria and Albert Museum, London)

*Fig. 7:* Plate of the "Rhodian" period.
(Museum für Kunsthandwerk, Frankfurt)

*Fig. 8:* Plate of the "Rhodian" period.
(Museum für Islamische Kunst, West Berlin)

*Fig. 9:* Plate of the "Rhodian" period.
(Benaki Museum, Athens)

*Fig. 10:* Plate of the "Rhodian" period.
(Benaki Museum, Athens)

*Fig. 11:* Plate of the "Rhodian" period.
(Musée des Arts Décoratifs, Paris)

*Fig. 12:* Plate of the "Rhodian" period.
(Benaki Museum, Athens)

XIII

*Fig. 13:* Long-necked bottle of the "Rhodian" period.
(British Museum, London)

*Fig. 14:* Long-necked bottle of the "Rhodian" period.
(British Museum, London)

*Fig. 15:* Vase of the "Rhodian" period.
(Victoria and Albert Museum, London)

*Fig. 16:* Jug of the "Rhodian" period.
(King Faisal Center, Kuwait)

Fig. 17: Jug of the blue-and-white period.
(Musée National de Céramique, Sèvres)

Fig. 19: Bowl of the "Rhodian" period.
(British Museum, London)

Fig. 20: Lidded bowl of the "Rhodian" period.
(British Museum, London)

Fig. 18: Tankard of the "Rhodian" period.
(Museum für Islamische Kunst, West Berlin)

Fig. 21: Jug of the "Rhodian" period.
(British Museum, London)

XV

# TREASURY OF TURKISH DESIGNS

*670 Motifs*
*from Iznik Pottery*

Designs typical of the "Damascus" period.

Designs typical of the "Rhodian" period.

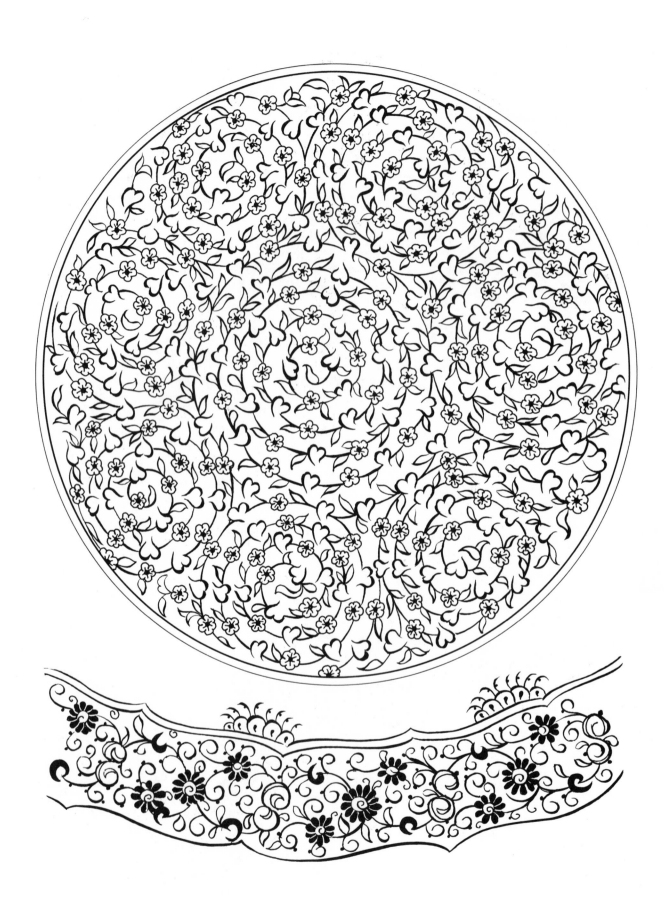

"Golden Horn" spiral designs, blue-and-white period.

Designs of the blue-and-white period, the lower example with repeated
Arabic inscriptions.

Floral motifs from the blue-and-white period.

Designs of the blue-and-white period.

Naturalistically painted Chinese-style vines and grapes, blue-and-white period.

Blue-turquoise-white period: further stylization of the motifs on the facing page.

9

Floral motifs from the blue-turquoise-white period.

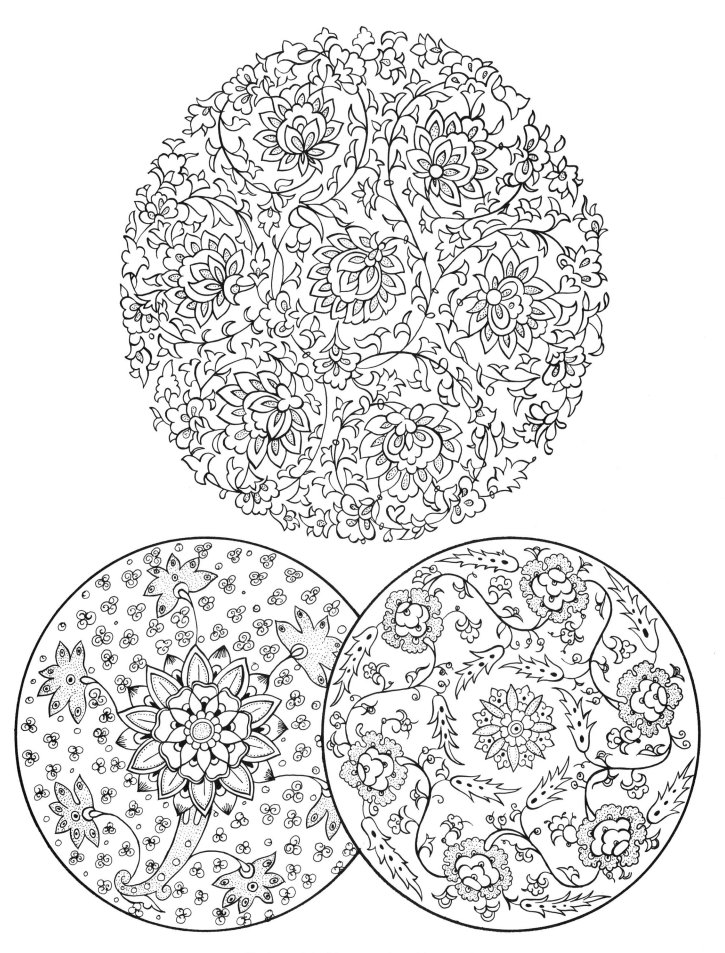

Designs of the blue-turquoise-white period.

Cloud scrolls, blue-and-white period.

Cloud scrolls, blue-and-white period.

Cloud motifs on vessels of later periods.

Cloud motifs on vessels of later periods.

Designs of the "Damascus" period, with flowers and *hatayi* motifs.

Designs of the "Damascus" period, with flowers and *hatayi* motifs.

Examples of the rounded type of *hatayi* floral motif, "Damascus" period.

"Damascus" design featuring rounded *hatayi* motifs.

Examples of the pointed type of *hatayi* floral motif, "Damascus" period.

"Damascus" design featuring *saz* leaf motifs and a pointed *hatayi* flower.

Seminaturalistic pomegranate motifs, "Damascus" period.

Seminaturalistic pomegranate motifs, "Damascus" period.

Designs incorporating pomegranate motifs, "Damascus" period.

Designs incorporating pomegranate motifs, "Damascus" period.

Naturalistic floral designs, "Rhodian" period.

Naturalistic floral designs, "Rhodian" period.

Tulips—a favorite Ottoman motif—as seen on Iznik pottery of all periods.

Tulips, all periods.

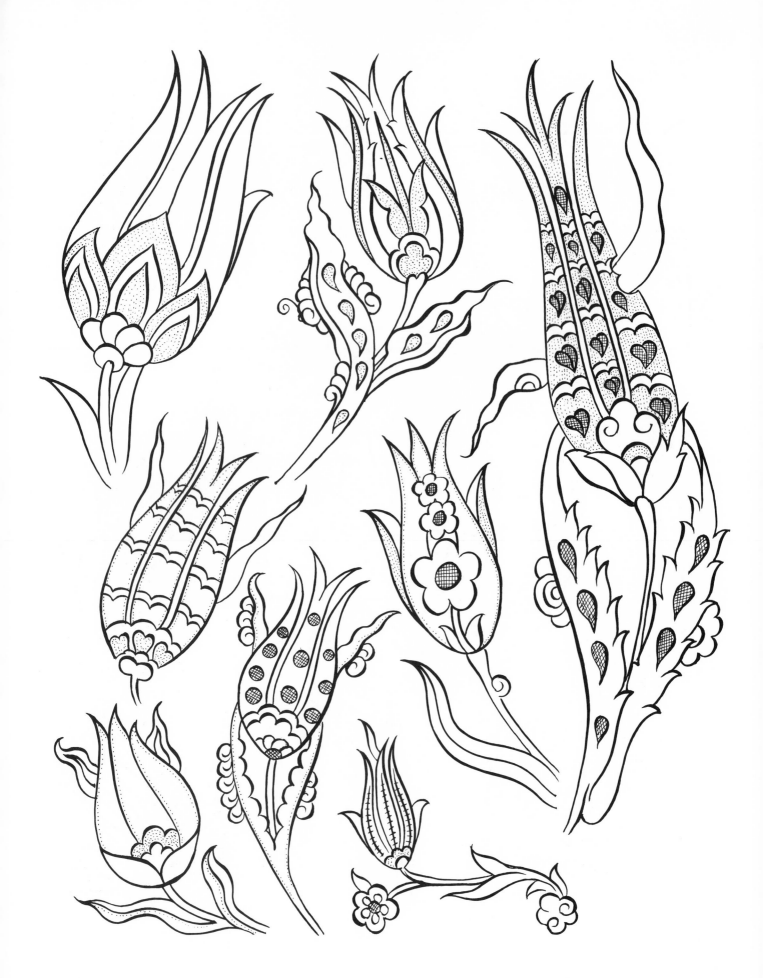

Tulips, all periods.

Tulips, all periods.

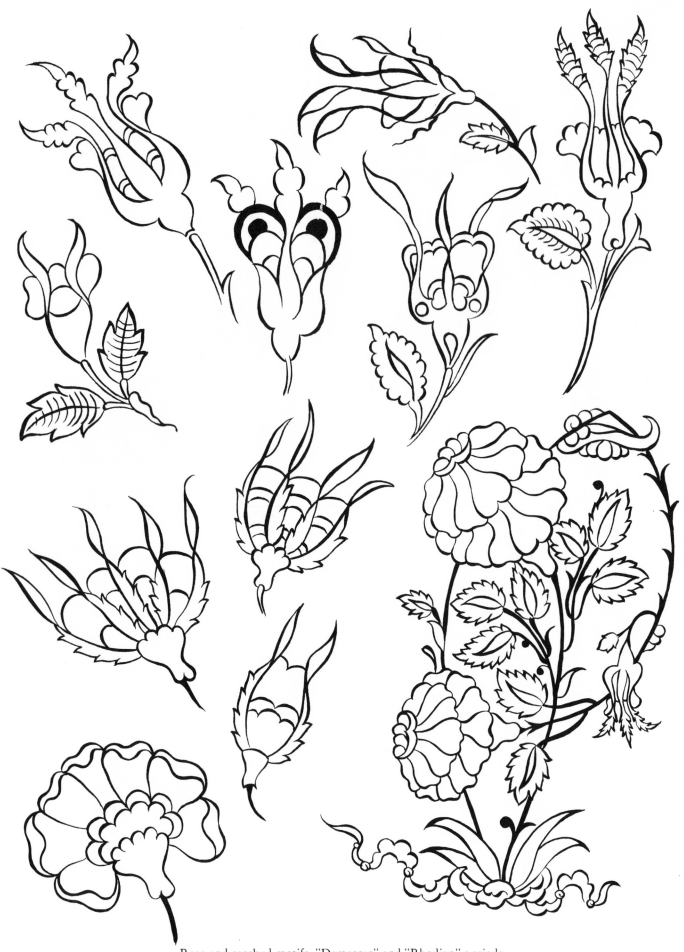

Rose and rosebud motifs, "Damascus" and "Rhodian" periods.

Rose and rosebud motifs, "Damascus" and "Rhodian" periods.

Carnation motifs, blue-turquoise-white and "Rhodian" periods.

Carnation motifs, blue-turquoise-white and "Rhodian" periods.

Designs featuring the cypress motif, "Rhodian" period.

Designs featuring the cypress motif, "Rhodian" period.

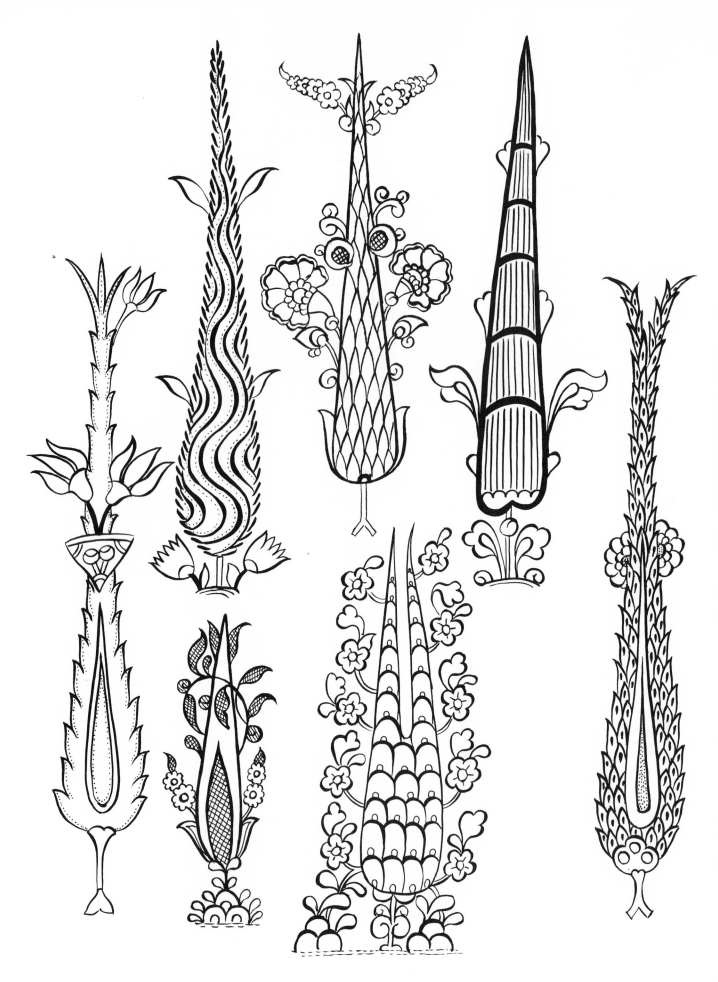

Cypress motifs from Iznik pottery of all periods.

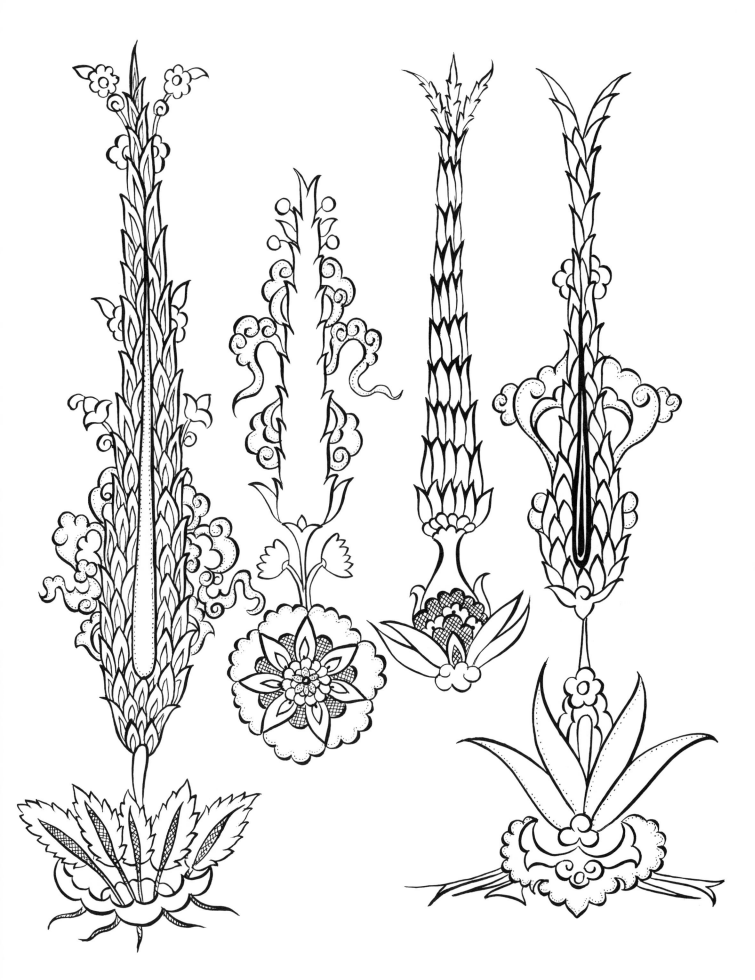

Cypress motifs, all periods.

Clusters, chiefly forming the bases of floral bouquets (at bottoms of plate designs).

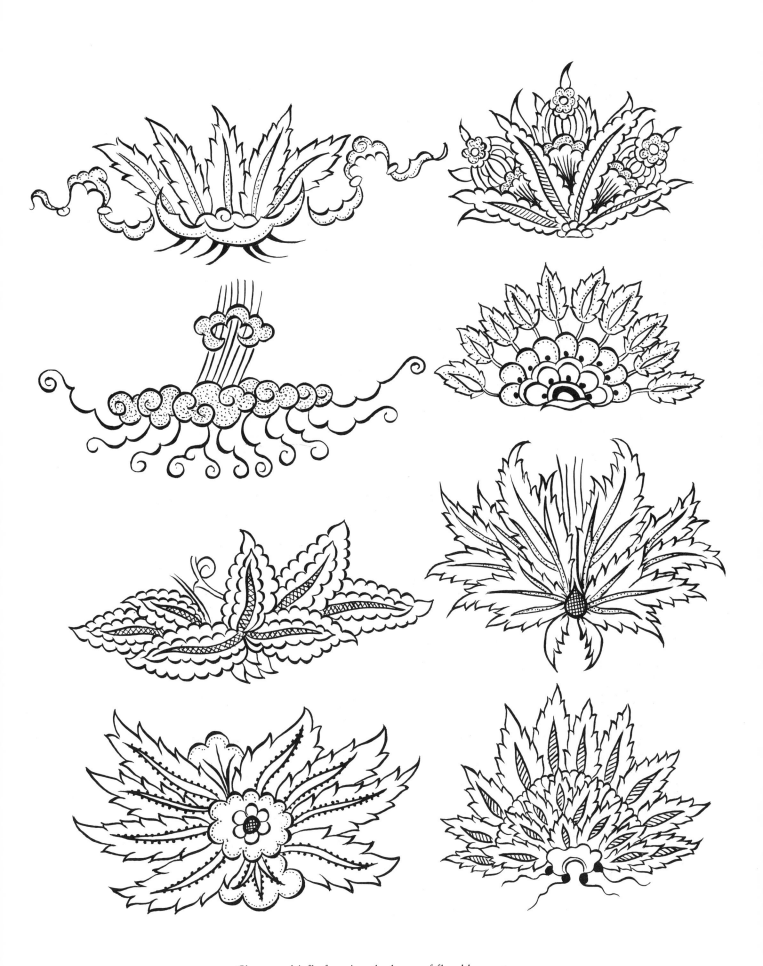

Clusters, chiefly forming the bases of floral bouquets.

41

Iris motifs, "Rhodian" period.

Various garden flowers, "Rhodian" period.

Hyacinths and similar flowers, "Damascus" and "Rhodian" periods.

44

Hyacinths and similar flowers, "Damascus" and "Rhodian" periods.

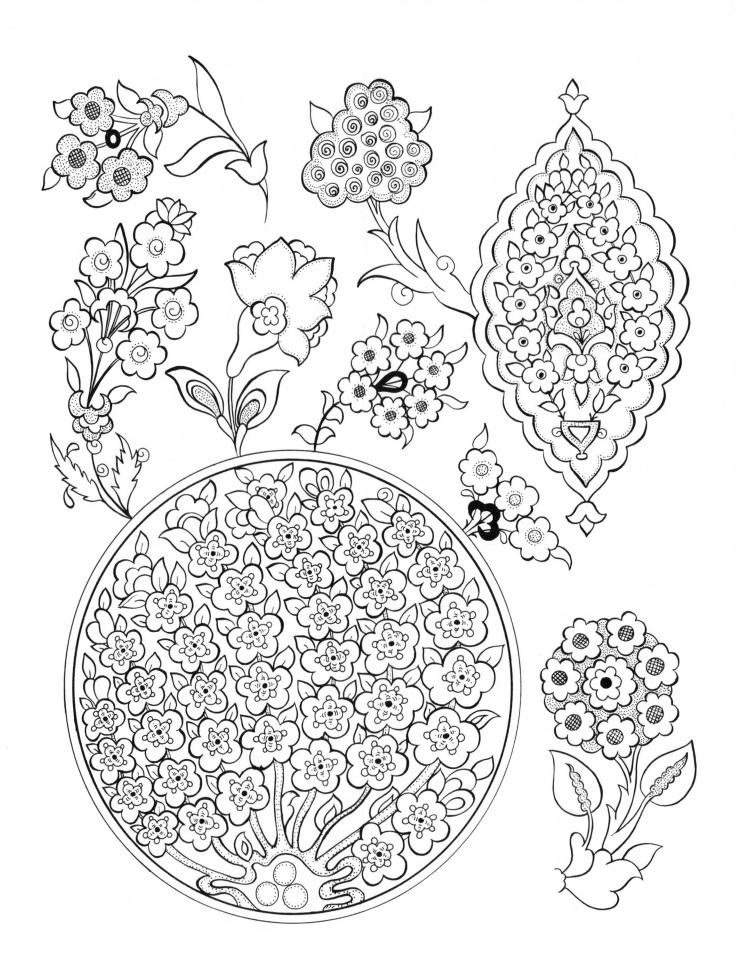

"Spring tree" and blossom motifs symbolizing eternal springtime, "Rhodian" period.

"Spring tree" and blossom motifs, "Rhodian" period.

Designs of the "Rhodian" period, the plate in the center showing the
dagger-leaf (*saz*) motif.

The *saz*, among the motifs most frequently used in the "Rhodian" period.

Details and variations of the *saz* motif, "Damascus" and "Rhodian" periods.

50

Variations of the *saz* motif, "Damascus" and "Rhodian" periods.

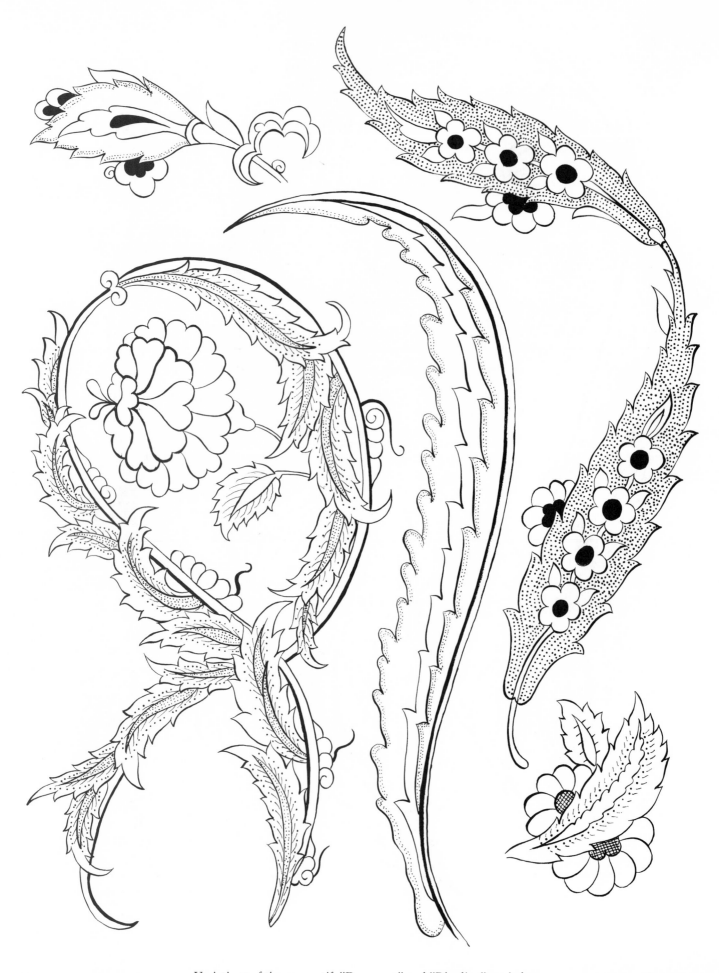

Variations of the *saz* motif, "Damascus" and "Rhodian" periods.

Variations of the *saz* motif, "Damascus" and "Rhodian" periods.

*Hatayi* motifs, "Rhodian" period.

*Hatayi* motifs, "Rhodian" period.

Designs with vase motifs, "Damascus" period.

Designs with vase motifs, "Rhodian" period.

Designs with small vase motifs, "Rhodian" period.

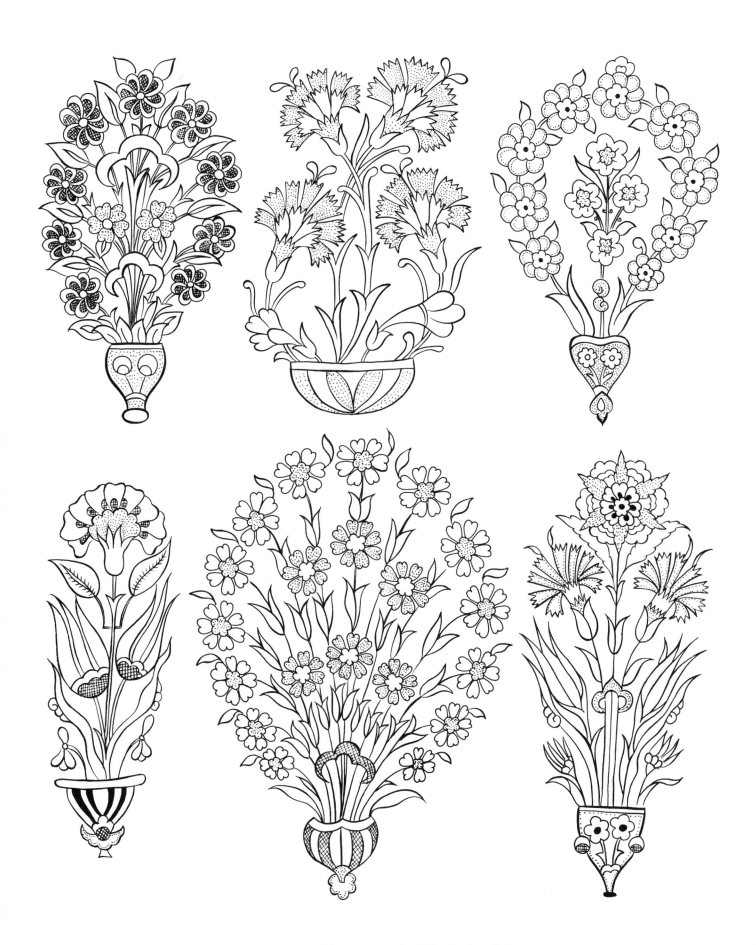

Small vase and bouquet motifs, "Rhodian" period.

Designs with holy-water flasks, seventeenth century.

Designs with holy-water flasks, seventeenth century.

61

Designs with intersecting *rumi* scrolls.

Designs with intersecting *rumi* scrolls.

Designs with *rumi* scrolls, "Rhodian" period.

*Rumi* scrolls: individual details and on the lid of a bowl of the "Rhodian" period.

Geometrical designs, "Rhodian" period.

Geometrically based designs, "Rhodian" period.

Designs with rosettes, "Rhodian" period.

Designs that radiate from a central point.

*Shamsah* **medallions** (motifs derived from manuscript painting).

Designs using *shamsah* medallions, "Rhodian" period.

Border designs, "Damascus" period.

Border designs, "Rhodian" period.

Border designs.

Border designs, chiefly using the rock-and-wave motif, "Damascus"
and "Rhodian" periods.

Designs using the *chintemani* motif (dot clusters), "Rhodian" period.

Designs using the *chintemani* motif, "Rhodian" period.

Designs with "fish scale" background, "Rhodian" period.

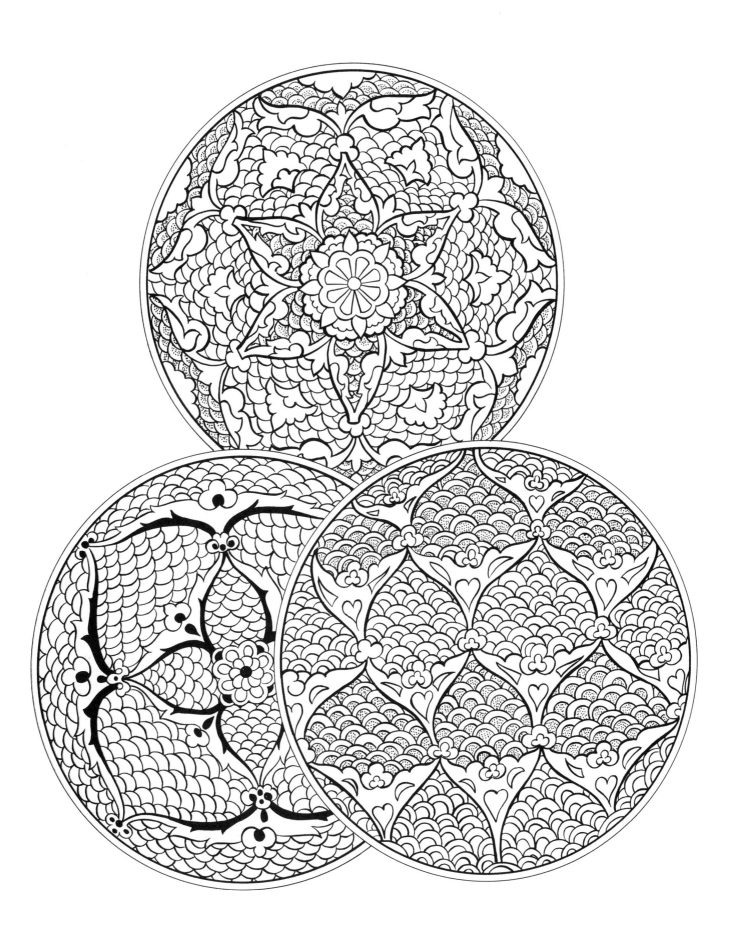

Designs with "fish scale" background, "Rhodian" period.

Designs using the "fish scale" motif (here resembling pinecones), "Rhodian" period.

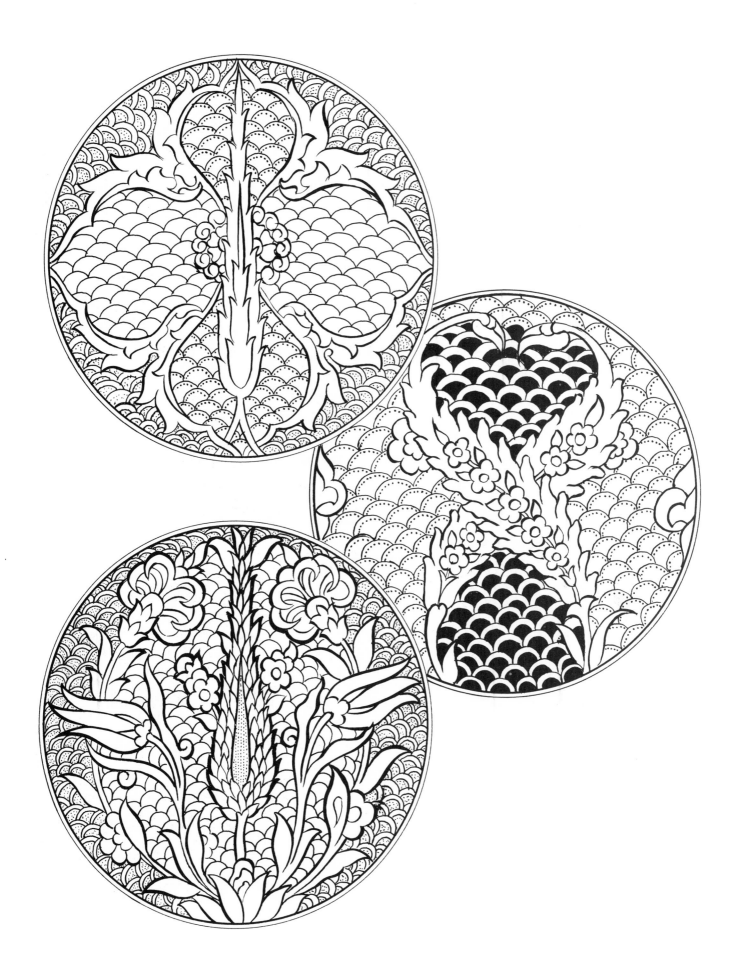

Designs using the "fish scale" motif, "Rhodian" period.

Designs using spiral background motifs called "snails," "Rhodian" period.

Plates from a set with identical border designs and spiral backgrounds but varying
inner designs, "Rhodian" period.

Sailing ship and galleon motifs, seventeenth century.

Sailing ship and galleon designs, seventeenth century.

Designs using several sailing ships, seventeenth century.

Designs using sailing ships, seventeenth century.

Designs using sailing ships and galleons, seventeenth century.

Designs using sailing ships and galleons, seventeenth century.

Designs using sailing ships, fish and human figures, seventeenth century.

Fish motifs, seventeenth century.

Bird motifs, "Rhodian" period.

Peacock motifs, symbolizing freedom and good luck, "Damascus" and "Rhodian" periods.

Bird design and motifs, "Rhodian" period.

Bird motifs, "Rhodian" period.

Designs using bird motifs, "Rhodian" period.

Designs using bird motifs, "Rhodian" period.

Lion motifs (including lion-and-sun), "Rhodian" period.

Lion design and motifs, "Rhodian" period.

Designs using animals, blue-turquoise-white period and seventeenth century.

Deer design and motifs, seventeenth century.

Animal design and motifs, seventeenth century.

Rabbit designs and motifs, seventeenth century.

Fabulous creatures (dragon and phoenix), seventeenth century.

Fabulous creatures (dragon and phoenix), seventeenth century.

Harpy motifs, seventeenth century.

Harpy and monkey designs and motifs, seventeenth century.

107

Human figures, seventeenth century.

Human figures, seventeenth century.

Human figures, seventeenth century.

Human figures, seventeenth century.